MERRY [barcode obscures text]

to

DAD

LOTS OF LOVE.

cameron ♡

SCOTTISH WIT

quips and quotes

TOM HAY

summersdale

SCOTTISH WIT

Summersdale Publishers Ltd
46 West Street
Chichester
West Sussex
PO19 1RP
UK

www.summersdale.com

Printed and bound in Singapore

ISBN: 978-1-84024-730-5

Contents

Editor's Note

With wit-smiths as illustrious as Robert Louis Stevenson, Robert Burns and Sir Arthur Conan Doyle, and a history more chequered than tartan, it is not surprising that the Scots have a special brand of humour.

Scots certainly aren't averse to turning the laugh round on themselves: take Billy Connolly's retort about the Scottish climate: 'There are two seasons in Scotland: June and winter.'

Within these pages you'll find sparkling Scottish witticisms on subjects as diverse as love and marriage, work and money, films and books, politics and sport – all guaranteed to make you laugh louder than a set of bagpipes.

Eating and Drinking

At least the haggis isn't a real animal.

Danny Bhoy

There is only one difference between a long life and a good dinner: that, in the dinner, the sweets come last.

Robert Louis Stevenson

Kippers – fish that like a lot of sleep.

Chic Murray

Pets, like their owners,
tend to expand a little over
the Christmas period.

Frances Wright

Freedom and whisky go together.

Robert Burns

My theory is that all of Scottish cuisine is based on a dare.

Mike Myers

Love and Marriage

Instead of getting married again, I'm going to find a woman I don't like and just give her a house.

Rod Stewart

Love may not make the world go round, but I must admit that it makes the ride worthwhile.

Sean Connery

Wives in their husbands' absences grow subtler, And daughters sometimes run off with the butler.

George Byron

Marriage is a wonderful invention: then again, so is a bicycle repair kit.

Billy Connolly

She had been married so often she bought a drip-dry wedding dress.

Chic Murray

Faces that have charmed us the most escape us the soonest.

Sir Walter Scott

Any time I get ideas above my station my wife says, 'Put the garbage out'.

Sandy Lyle

You only require two things in life: your sanity and your wife.

Tony Blair

Of all ghosts the ghosts of our old loves are the worst.

Sir Arthur Conan Doyle

Marriage is one long conversation, chequered by disputes.

Robert Louis Stevenson

*Marriages are all happy,
it's having breakfast
together that causes
most of the trouble.*

Scottish proverb

Bonny Scotland

I don't know if Alex McLeish knows whether I'm Scottish or not. Maybe I'll have to put 'Mac' in front of my surname.

Chris Iwelumo

Scotsmen are metaphysical and emotional, they are sceptical and mystical, they are romantic and ironic, they are cruel and tender, and full of mirth and despair.

William Dunbar

In Scotland, when people congregate, they tend to argue and discuss and reason; in Orkney, they tell stories.

George Mackay Brown

There are two seasons in Scotland: June and winter.

Billy Connolly

A Scots pessimist is a man who feels badly when he feels good for fear he'll feel worse when he feels better.

Scottish proverb

We are undoubtedly a sentimental people, and it sometimes plays havoc with that other celebrated sense of ours, the practical.

J. M. Barrie

... being typically undemonstrative Scots, our reunion on home soil wasn't marked with any great show of emotion – just a plethora of broad smiles.

Peter Kerr, *From Paella to Porridge*

The Scots are steadfast – not their clime.

Thomas Crawford

*There are few more impressive
sights in the world than a
Scotsman on the make.*

J. M. Barrie

*... the past clings like
sand to wet feet.*

Geddes MacGregor on the Scottish

Being a Scotsman through and through, Jock was compelled to try his best for that cut-price deal, even if it meant he'd end up being out of pocket by clinching it.

Peter Kerr, *A Basketful of Snowflakes*

Work and
Money

Work is the meat of life,

pleasure the dessert.

B. C. Forbes

… he'll do nothing which might damage his career.

J. M. Barrie on the grandest moral attribute of a Scotsman

… the only machine I ever understood was a wheelbarrow, and that but imperfectly.

E. T. Bell

It is not real work unless you would rather be doing something else.

J. M. Barrie

Don't meddle with other people's ideas when you have all the work cut out for you in trying to express your own.

Charles Rennie Mackintosh

There is more credit and satisfaction in being a first-rate truck driver than a tenth-rate executive.

B. C. Forbes

Sport

*As a small boy I was torn
between two ambitions:
to be a footballer or to
run away and join a
circus. At Partick Thistle
I got to do both.*

Alan Hansen

The standard of sweet trolleys at the team get-togethers.

Pat Nevin after being asked what was the greatest improvement in Scottish football in the past ten years

On one hole I'm like Arnold Palmer, and then at the next I'm Lilli Palmer.

Sean Connery on his golfing skills

Some people think football is a matter of life and death, I assure you, it's much more serious than that.

Bill Shankly

If it came to a toss-up between golf and the movies, I'd pick golf.

Sean Connery

Golf is an indispensable adjunct to high civilization.

Andrew Carnegie on leaving a large sum of money to Yale University to build a golf course

I love what rugby is – brain as well as brawn, and then beer together afterwards.

Roy Laidlaw

Golf is an awkward set of bodily contortions designed to produce a graceful result.

Tommy Armour

In my sport the quick are too often listed among the dead.

Jackie Stewart

Half a million for Remi Moses? You could get the original Moses for that, and the tablets as well.

Tommy Docherty

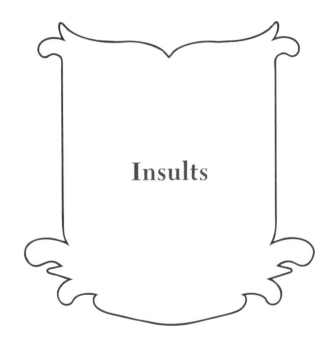

Insults

Couldn't we sponsor Bros not to get back together?

Gordon Brown on raising funds for charity

Nobody thought Mel Gibson could play a Scot but look at him now! Alcoholic and a racist!

Frankie Boyle

John Barnes's problem is that he gets injured appearing on A Question of Sport.

Tommy Docherty

Leonardo DiCaprio is patently the result of an unnatural act of passion between William Hague and Piglet from Babe.

A. A. Gill

The great thing about Glasgow is that if there's a nuclear attack it'll look exactly the same afterwards.

Billy Connolly

I think PR is a ridiculous job. They are the head lice of civilization.

A. A. Gill

She was a large woman who seemed not so much dressed as upholstered.

J. M. Barrie

Ally MacLeod thinks that tactics are a new kind of mint.

Billy Connolly

The last time I saw something like that, it was crawling out of Sigourney Weaver's stomach.

Ally McCoist on David Bowman of Dundee United

**Scottish
Proverbs**

*How do you disperse
an angry Scottish mob?
Nae bother – just take
up a collection.*

A trout in the pot is better than a salmon in the sea.

What butter and whisky will not cure, there is no cure for.

Twelve highlanders and a bagpipe make a rebellion.

To marry is to halve your rights and double your duties.

*Scotsmen take all they can get
– and a little more if they can.*

*Three failures and a fire
make a Scotsman's fortune.*

*Land of the hill
and heather
Land of the awful weather
Land where the midges
gather – Scotland
the brave.*

*Get what you can and
keep what you have; that's
the way to get rich.*

*Never marry for money,
ye'll borrow it cheaper.*

Wise Words

He who has provoked the lash of wit, cannot complain that he smarts from it.

James Boswell

Nothing can confound a wise man more than laughter from a dunce.

George Byron

*We are all failures; at least,
all the best of us are.*

J. M. Barrie

*Time makes fools of us all.
Our only comfort is that
greater shall come after us.*

E. T. Bell

It is not every man who can be exquisitely miserable, any more than exquisitely happy.

James Boswell

As we grow older we escape from the tyranny of matter and recognise that the true centre of gravity is the mind.

John Buchan

Poor is the triumph o'er the timid hare!

James Thomson

Problems are only opportunities with thorns on them.

Hugh Miller

Temptations come, as a general rule, when they are sought.

Margaret Oliphant

Never trust a man who, when left alone in a room with a tea cosy, doesn't try it on.

Billy Connolly

Fame and
the Arts

To be occasionally quoted is the only fame I care for.

Alexander Smith

A page of my journal is like a cake of portable soup. A little may be diffused into a considerable portion.

James Boswell

If a farmer fills his barn with grain, he gets mice. If he leaves it empty, he gets actors.

Sir Walter Scott

*By the usual reckoning,
the worst books make
the best films.*

Iain Banks

People may say that what I do is really clever, but it's not really at all. It's not Swift.

Rory Bremner

I know not, sir, whether Bacon wrote the works of Shakespeare, but if he did not it seems to me that he missed the opportunity of his life.

J. M. Barrie

I make it a rule to cheat on nobody but booksellers, a race on whom I have no mercy.

Sir Walter Scott

When an idea is dead it is embalmed in a textbook.

Sir Patrick Geddes

No human being ever spoke of scenery for above two minutes at a time, which makes me suspect that we hear too much of it in literature.

Robert Louis Stevenson

I'm just looking for that moment to drop my Jedi knickers and pull out my real light sabre.

Ewan McGregor on filming *Star Wars*

It is all very well to be able to write books, but can you waggle your ears?

J. M. Barrie

Books are good enough in their own way, but they are a mighty bloodless substitute for life.

Robert Louis Stevenson

If you didn't join for the girls, choose another profession.

Tom Conti on acting

Books are like a mirror. If an ass looks in, you can't expect an angel to look out.

B. C. Forbes

*I have always hated
that damn James Bond.
I'd like to kill him.*

Sean Connery

Life

Life's more amusing
than we thought.

Andrew Lang

*A well-written life
is almost as rare as
a well-spent one.*

Thomas Carlyle

You can't live on amusement.
It is the froth on water – an
inch deep and then the mud.

George MacDonald

No man can become a
saint in his sleep.

Henry Drummond

The life of every man is a diary in which he means to write one story, and writes another.

J. M. Barrie

I am prepared to go anywhere, provided it be forward.

David Livingstone

It is better to lose health
like a spendthrift than
to waste it like a miser.

Robert Louis Stevenson

Age is not all decay; it is the ripening, the swelling, of the fresh life within, that withers and bursts the husk.

George MacDonald

The dominant thought of youth is the bigness of the world, of age its smallness.

John Buchan

Life is a long lesson
in humility.

J. M. Barrie

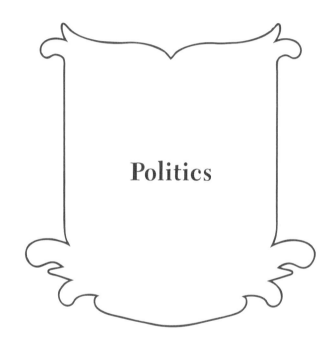

Politics

I did maths for a year at university. I don't think I was very good at it. And some people would say it shows.

Gordon Brown

I think that I shall not long have anything to do with the House of Commons again – I never saw so many wrong-headed people on all sides gathered together.

James Watt

Politics is the enemy of the imagination.

Ian McEwan

The cabinet has been shaken about a bit, but it's the same old jar of jellybeans.

David Steel

Politics now is rather like going into Starbucks for a coffee.

Rory Bremner

He probably just thinks Tony Blair's put on weight and had a mild stroke.

Frankie Boyle wondering whether George Bush knows who Gordon Brown is

They are going backwards. They have now skipped a generation. At this rate the next leader will have to be exhumed.

Rory Bremner on the Conservatives after
Michael Howard was made leader

We spend more on cows than on the poor.

Gordon Brown

Stuff and Nonsense

I really want to play Princess Leia and stick some big pastries on my head.

Ewan McGregor

To shake your rump is to be environmentally aware.

David Byrne

A cement mixer collided with a prison van... Motorists are asked to be on the lookout for 16 hardened criminals.

Ronnie Corbett

If America had been discovered as many times as I have, no one would remember Columbus.

Sean Connery

I am sure of nothing so little as my own intentions.

George Byron

There were so many holes in my socks I could put them on in seventeen different ways.

Chic Murray

I don't know why I should have to learn algebra... I'm never likely to go there.

Billy Connolly

Who discovered we could get milk from cows, and what did he think he was doing at the time?

Billy Connolly

A neighbour put his budgerigar in the mincing machine and invented shredded tweet.

Chic Murray

I'm Britain's worst dressed man. I am to style what Jeremy Clarkson is to lesbian peace-loving organic whole food meditation collectives.

Andrew Marr apologises for his infamous pink top

www.summersdale.com